HELP!

I'm Homeschooling!

Helpful Habits for the
Heart of Homeschooling

TRICIA HODGES

hodgepodgemom.com

Dedication

This book is dedicated to each and every one of my fellow homeschool mamas. I pray that those of you who read my words will know that it is all worth it! You CAN homeschool. The investment and the rewards are so very rich. My hope is in return you will stay the course and one day invest in the lives of other parents and "urge the younger women to love their husbands and children..." in the model of Titus 2.

Introduction

In this book, I'm sharing my very best, practical and easy-to-implement habits with you. As mothers, we are often living in survival mode, responding to the urgent. My desire is for you to have the help and the tools you need for day to day homeschooling and parenting. I want you to find that strong foundation of habits so that you and your homeschool will thrive – even when the storms come and the hormones hit. Coffee and chocolate sure help. Even when you, bless your heart, have to reheat that coffee three times throughout the day. I am here to tell you that a firm foundation and an arsenal of habits help hold things together and bless the whole family. There's a sense of freedom and security with habits. Be encouraged my fellow homeschool mamas! You will see the fruits of your efforts and prayers.

Blessings,

Tricia

Contents

Helpful Habits for the Heart of Homeschooling

For about two decades we've turned to our habits as the 'bones' of our day. Our habits help us with everything from a basic school day to getting food on the table. We narrowed our focus by leaning on one or two habits more heavily when all the children were age 10 and under. Over the years, we've tweaked habits to meet our needs with growing children. So with babies, toddlers, stacks of school books, hungry mouths and now towering teens, these are the basic routes we've discovered for seeing results.

You may be thinking: We can usually handle the basic reading, writing and arithmetic. But what about brushing teeth? How do I find balance with a roaming toddler? Or, perhaps you are wondering how do we fit in science and history? Before we get to school subjects, let's start with the habits meeting the heart of homeschooling.

Now you are thinking: How do I make habits stick?... Are you kidding me? How can I even start to build a habit with all that is going on in my home?

How to Prepare Your Heart for Homeschooling

I have found making habits stick is easier than you might imagine. You simply have to start by forming habits for yourself.

1. **Pray.** It is amazing how often I try to do things in my own power. Please friends, remember to turn to the source of strength. Ask. Bring it all – everything – to Him.

2. **Pick One Habit to Build.** Why not start with one, simple habit a month. Just adding one habit per month beats the overwhelm and makes it doable. Master the one habit and then address another when you are ready.

2. **Think practically.** Be easy on yourself. Pick a habit that works into your day. Start perhaps with something you already do that you would like to do better.

3. **Make it fun.** Two of our longest running family habits were built around the supper table. We all have to eat, right? Start with fun habits like those I share in the following chapter on the Habit of Celebrating.

Throughout this book I share several of the basic habits of you can consider for your homeschool day. **Remember, these habits were ones worked on one at a time over several years.** I encourage you to pick the one that you feel will bless your homeschool the most. Gently fold it into your homeschool day.

The best thing that you can give your children, next to good habits, is good memories. ~Barbara Johnson

Hodgepodge Hint: Summer is a GREAT time to build a new habit.

What I Wish I'd Known When I Started Homeschooling

Dear Homeschooler,

There were so many titles I could have given this list: Encouragement for all Homeschoolers, 10 Pieces of Advice for a New Homeschooler, What I Wish I'd Known When I Started Homeschooling, My Best Advice, Don't Let Homeschooling Get You Down. Whatever the title, I hope you find something amidst this advice to urge you on.

God will fill in the 'gaps'.

He has designed each of your children with specific gifts and talents. Each unique. And He says, "I know what I'm doing. I have it all planned out—plans to take care of you, not abandon you, plans to give you the future you hope for" in Jeremiah 29:11.

Major in the three Rs in the younger years.

Reading, writing and arithmetic. Read, read, read. Snuggle up on the couch. Work on phonics, simple math problems. Build those skills because everything else grows from those basics. A solid foundation in reading, writing and arithmetic is important. Don't get distracted by shiny boxes of curriculum.

Wait on formal science until 3rd grade.

This advice was given to me by fellow mothers in my homeschool group. I whole-heartedly agree! There will be plenty of time for formal science. In the meantime, go to the library and load up on books on a science subject your child is interested in.

Enjoy growing a love for God's world through regular nature study. I remember back to when my older two were both under three years old, science studies meant dropping a leaf and watching it float down the stream. When it rained, we built a tin foil boat and watched it float around the curb in the cul-de-sac. Simple discoveries that help a child enjoy the outdoors enhance a love for both the science and wonder of God's world.

Act like homeschoolers.

Learn from me and don't try to reproduce a school setting at home. Make learning natural and comfortable. Build learning centers. We are often changing up our homeschool and rearranging furniture to meet needs with the goal of making learning easy. Move your learning outside on a nice day. Take advantage of the freedoms in your schedule.

Don't skip Bible study and quiet time with the Lord for academics. (And that includes mom!)

Teach to the heart. Devotionals and Bible studies are built into our curriculum budget. Aim to keep God's word within easy reach.

Life is messy. Habits help.

Slowly build habits that help your homeschool day so you will have practical support to lean on.

Stress life skills.

The goal is for our children to be responsible, God-fearing adults. Let your children learn the stuff of real life while at home. Let them fail under your care. Drive the lawn mower. Plan the menu or the making of afternoon snacks.

Enjoy activities close by.

Especially when my children were little, I would worry over the fact that I was not taking them on *all* the field trips. But, we visited my grandmother every week. We also enjoyed many backyard nature studies! Go to the farmer's market. Walk the little trail down the road. An outing doesn't have to be hard or take much time – especially when your children are all little.

Laugh.

Especially laugh when doing math. When you want to scream, just sing.

Prayer throughout the day.

If your children develop the habit of prayer then they will always have the answers.

The Habit of Prayer

The community helpers puzzle. Its pieces dumped in the floor, *again*. I find myself frustrated, *again*.

Frustrated to pick up the pieces and frustrated we were all sick. Frustrated we couldn't get out and help the victims of recent flooding.

But the Lord calmly gave me an answer, in His patient way. As I was picking up each puzzle piece, He said, "*Pray.*"

The ambulance piece – pray for ambulance workers. The police car – pray for our police force rescuing flood victims. The tow truck – wow. I hadn't even thought about all those cars needing to be towed away. And look, the school bus.

I adore practical answers.

As a young mother, I thought I was supposed to go off to my little corner and have my quiet time. More and more that became a hard thing to do. I didn't quite understand how I was supposed to pray without ceasing.

I imagined myself, face down, in the middle of the floor trying to pray and acting oblivious to children running all around me, hollering, "Mama!" "Ma*ma*!" Me, answering, "Quiet now children, I'm praying."

The Lord has gently taught me that prayer should be the foundation of our day. Not a separate practice, not always apart from the children. Though there certainly is a time for formal prayer, the praying habit is to be passed on. It's a way of life.

I once heard prayer compared to breathing. Breathe out… send a prayer up… Breathe in…soak up His wisdom, give thanks. It's a conversation. *It's easy.* Something you don't even have to put effort into.

Pray without ceasing. I Thessalonians 5:17

Guess what? I've found freedom in praying out loud while driving my homeschool "bus" to activities. "Lord, help us to be safe. Help children to obey. Help us to be polite and have a good time."

Yes, I enjoy quiet time before the children wake. But the children should also catch me with my Bible when they come down the steps, all sleepy-eyed, in the morning. "Here, child, bring that warm blanket and snuggle with me. Let's have some quiet time with Jesus."

Other practical prayers as you go about your day:

- When you hear a siren, stop and pray with the children. Pray not only for those that might be hurting but also for those that are responding to the emergency. Pray for healing. Siren prayers usually prompt us to pray for others we know with urgent needs.
- When that airplane flies overhead pray, "God, please bless the people in the airplane." My mother taught us this simple prayer.
- Can't find something? Pray. The simple act of stopping and praying for wisdom helps calm everybody down.

"Mama, shouldn't we pray?" the seven-year-old reminds.
We do. And then I find my keys.

Simple, anytime prayers:

- "Help!"
- "Please give me wisdom!"
- "Allow me to show love."

Just pray. All day. Amen.

You can't change what you have or haven't done over the past year. Just start where you are, ask the Lord to make you a "joyful mother of children," pray for grace and wisdom (and strength and patience), and move forward. – Vicki Bentley

The Habit of Homeschool Planning and Goal Setting

In repentance and rest you will be saved, in quietness and trust is your strength… Isaiah 30:15

As mothers we sometimes live in the urgent. This hungry child, that weepy one, another needing a push on the swing…

However, it's beneficial to step out of the urgent into the quiet. It is so very helpful to step out of our regular spot and look to our source of strength. Make some quiet time a priority. Jesus set the example. (*At daybreak, Jesus went out to a solitary place* Luke 4: 42).

Once a year I purposefully take the time to think on each of my five children. I set aside a special time to make goals for the next year. Homeschool goals, a life skills assessment, but most importantly time in prayer for each child. How is she doing spiritually? How can we give him a bit more of challenge in this subject? What do I imagine this child to be like as an adult? And, yes, I did say we'd potty train over the summer.

I do my goal setting and planning while on family vacation but save the work for home. I bring along my current favorite spiral notebook and pen. And I rise early and meet with the Lord over matters. Maybe on your own turf you can steal away to the back porch or front step.

In the past I spent an hour just one morning. You'd be surprised the thoughts you can record in one quiet, early-morning hour before the rest of the house wakes. Other years I decided ahead of time I'd spread my planning over five days. That equals a planning session for one child each weekday.

I really anticipate this annual planning time. I've seen the results. Been surprised at what the Lord puts in my head.

I start with prayer. I thank God for my child. I thank Him for the privilege of parenting and teaching. I ask again for wisdom. (Oh, that is daily!) I gaze on the sunrise, sip my coffee, **and I write down** what comes to mind.

Goal Setting for the Children

Listen and allow the Lord to fill in the blanks for you. Here's a sample of how mine goes:

> …yes, at this age I was already practicing driving in the neighborhood. Maybe we just let her drive from the mailbox to the garage like her cousin does.

> …that typing practice website would be a fun thing to add in again even this month.

> …yes, it's time to remind ourselves about good table manners.

> …two middle-schoolers this school year, hmmm, we need to focus on even more independent work.

> …what about those preschool activity bags I was so keen on? How can we roll those type things in to our schedule? It has to be easy.

...how can we, as parents, help develop this child's interest and skill by investing in lessons or supplies?

Next, I spend a bit of time praying through needs for each of my children. I keep all my thoughts tucked in my spiral notebook. Later, when I am in the thick of weekly school planning, I pull out my list and incorporate the inspiration.

Goal Setting for Mama

Another time during the week I think over some goals for myself and the family. Goal setting doesn't have to be daunting or elaborate. For example, on the drive home from vacation, while the children had their headphones on, my husband and I chatted about the years ahead. We dreamed and set some goals. Here's a sample of mine:

- I wrote out the years through our youngest child's graduation. Together, we marveled at what age we'd all be and how quickly it will surely all pass.
- We dreamed of where we might go on anniversary trips for milestone anniversaries.
- We planned three fall birthday parties, made a list of house updates/projects for that year and wrote down ideas for Christmas presents for all the children.

Maybe there is a hobby you'd like to start or get back to? How about that stack of books on your nightstand? Start small and plan now. All of the family benefits when Mama practices continuing education.

Just 15 minute slices of goal setting each day will get you started.

The best part is now the inspiration is all out of my head and on the calendar or in my spiral notebook. There is less distraction in my mama brain so I can handle the day-to-day urgent. Being in a quiet spot for even 15 minutes really helps with planning. Being open to the Lord's guidance and direction is key.

> *We should make plans – counting on God to direct us.*
> Proverbs 16:9

Hodgepodge Hints:

- If you are in a stage of early risers, you can anticipate maybe 15-30 minutes of planning each morning. Know ahead of time you may be interrupted. It's ok. God places those appointments for a reason too.
- You might even be able to arrange for a morning away from your usual homeschool routine.
- You could take late evening walks with your husband after the children are tucked in bed and discuss the same type thoughts about your future.

The Habit of a Weekly Homeschool Planning Meeting

After the habit of annual goal setting and planning, and once you are in the nitty gritty of week-to-week homeschool, you can make plans weekly. If your children are all very young, then a weekly homeschool planning time might be a habit you build on your own. You may want to include your husband and talk about the week ahead. As your children grow older, a weekly homeschool planning meeting with all of your ages will help you get an outline for the week ahead. There are so many benefits to this time together.

> *Let all things be done decently and in order.*
> 1 Corinthians 14:40

How a Weekly Homeschool Planning Meeting Works

- The meeting takes anywhere from half an hour to an hour depending on the week ahead.
- My husband and I lead the meeting. It is so very helpful to have my husband, the principal of our homeschool, there to give us all guidance. He sometimes reminds the children that He is the head of our homeschool and that while he is away at work during the day, he leaves me in charge. So, ultimately, we all answer to him. That is such a blessing when we run into a character issue – or problem with a math concept.

- We might meet in the family room or at the kitchen table so that our resources are within easy reach.
- Our meetings happen on a Sunday afternoon so that my husband can be there. On occasion we have a meeting on a Monday morning when we have had a very busy and full Sunday.
- Everyone gathers their personal planners.
- At each weekly meeting we first go over what we will be learning together during the week.
- The younger ones are often playing quietly while we talk. The further along in the meeting we get, the younger ones are allowed to leave to play elsewhere. Then my husband and I can discuss plans with our middle and high schoolers.

The Benefits of a Weekly Homeschool Planning Meeting Habit

- Guidelines and recorded goals for the week are entered into individual planners.
- We go over the upcoming calendar with all the commitments and activities – together.
- There is no confusion over expectations for the week ahead.
- We have something to keep us on track in the midst of the craziness of the week.
- There is ownership when assignments are written down.
- Our students are given the chance to best manage their time independently and rearrange to suit their needs.
- Boundaries often bring out character issues in myself and my children. These are tough but much needed life lessons (e.g., yes, that assignment needs

to be finished even though there is that fun thing planned for that day on the calendar.)

- Consequences – both good and bad!

Yes we:

- Sometimes have a reluctant planner
- Have plans that change
- Get sidetracked
- Allow for spontaneous homeschool learning

This is a weekly time with parents to plan, review, discuss and consult. **Ultimately, planning is a gift of learning independence, wouldn't you say?**

Hodgepodge Hint: About 5th grade is a great time to start a child with a student planner.

The Habit of Date Night

When it is just Wednesday and it has already been a full week, I start to think of date night. Date night is just a little bit of time away with my husband. A breath of fresh air. A new perspective. And a better wife, better mama for it.

See, when you exchanged vows, you and your husband became a family. You were a family before children. Before homeschooling. Before all the activities you are currently committed to. Just the two of you.

Date night is a habit that my husband and I try to keep up at least once a week. Either a date night at home or going out the frugal way. Spending time with your spouse without the children around is crucial to a good marriage. Your affection for each other is part of your children's overall security. In short, while it seems you're doing it for the two of you, you're also doing it for them.

Is it worth the investment, worth the planning, worth the time and effort? Yes! **I encourage you. Build the habit of date night** – or a lunch date on a Saturday. Whatever works best for your schedule and your family. You and your husband will be blessed. Your children will be blessed too because they will see the priority you make of your marriage.

> *Trust steadily in God, hope unswervingly, love extravagantly. And the best of the three is love.* 1 Corinthians 13:13

I urge you. I charge you. Date your husband. I promise you. You will love it.

> **Hodgepodge Hint:** How to plan date nights? Maybe you daydream while washing dishes and then jot down a list of ideas. It is also nice for you and your husband to brainstorm about some local places you would like to visit. An inexpensive for dinner and a stroll together at a local park. Weather not great? Grab a drive thru hot chocolate and just go on a drive. It's just such great talking time!

The Habit of Teaching Multiple Ages

As homeschool mamas and parents, we can all learn from and help each other. I hope that some part of this habit of teaching multiple ages will bless you – whether you are balancing the needs of an age range or just starting your homeschool journey. I am imagining you and I sitting down for a visit. Would you like coffee or tea?

And while each of our homeschools and families are different, let me introduce you to our homeschool. Here at Hodgepodge we teach multiple ages. For a long time, I've called our homeschool learning method "Layers and Levels of Learning". That one-room schoolhouse type of learning. But ultimately, I've come to determine that Lasagna Learning describes it much more accurately.

Lasagna Learning

A Hodgepodge Recipe for Lasagna Learning: In this book I'm sharing the ingredients, the instructions for teaching multiple ages. It's a simple recipe, really. The recipe goes something like this:

Place a layer of learning in the pot (like my favorite slow cooker), add another layer, season with sauce, add another layer. Keep alternating layers until it is appetizing. Cook well, seasoned with spices. It's irresistible! Fill your plate of learning high! Little ones learning from older ones. Middle ones keeping things lively, always asking questions.

Not only do we have an age range here, we also have a wide range of learning styles. The temperature and conditions in which we serve our lasagna varies! See if you have any matching these descriptions:

- Two of our daughters learn by reading and are **visual learners**. They each choose to curl up with a book and learn independently.
- Our sons are **auditory learners**. They will listen to anything. So audio books and online learning are the way to go.
- Our Middle Girl could make, create, display, concoct, play, dialogue – she's a hands-on, **kinesthetic learner**.
- If you need help with determining your child's learning style, *The Way They Learn* is a great resource. Find this resource listed in my Favorite Resources section.

We homeschooling parents need to be aware and teaching to not only ages and ability but also to the different ways learning styles mesh together. So each child soaks up the rich vitamins of knowledge.

I must start by encouraging you. I *do not* do it all. We *do not* fit it all in. And I must remind you– there are seasons in this homeschool life. When I was smack in the middle of having babies, we did well to simply get the basics in. Just the three Rs – reading, writing and arithmetic.

> *If you don't know what you're doing, pray to the Father. He loves to help. You'll get his help, and won't be condescended to when you ask for it. Ask boldly, believingly, without a second thought.* James 1: 1-5, (The Message)

Hodgepodge Hint: How to start a homeschool day with a household? Get up before the children and get on your knees. I encourage you – impress upon you – start your day with some quiet prayer time. Wow, what 15 minutes of alone time in the morning or late at night can do for a mama! It's good to keep a daily habit of stepping out of the urgent, into the quiet, out of our regular spot and look to our Source of strength.

How to Start a Homeschool Routine with Little Ones

In all our years of starting to homeschool little ones, we have found that we can do the 'school work' in about an hour. **The important thing is to break the school subject time into short increments: 15 minutes here, a fun break, fifteen minutes there, a snack.** Later in the day – a read aloud in the afternoon or even at bedtime.

Start by making the little ones' routine all a natural part of your day. Here is a simple run down of what a typical morning might look like for our preschooler or younger elementary-aged child.

- We start with our Before School Checklist. These are simple reminders to brush your teeth, have some quiet time, make your bed, get dressed. Yes, sometimes we all need these basic reminders.
- Next, I sit in between our younger two and read Bible stories. Preschooler does some coloring in his Bible stories coloring book.
- Meanwhile, first grader works on the math calendar.
- When preschooler finishes up his Bible coloring, he might join in math time, playing with the math manipulative teddy bear counters first grader and I are using.
- Preschooler then enjoys one page of a preschool workbook.

Here we might take a break. Have a snack. Go outside and get a push on the swing, run or kick a ball. Notice the ants. Look up and soak up the sunshine.

- We pick back up with some short phonics practice.
- Next comes handwriting practice. Preschooler is practicing his name. First grader practices daily with her handwriting curriculum.
- To round out the day, our younger children join in short, age-appropriate doses the remainder of afternoon. This might include art, read aloud time and nature study.

Hodgepodge Hint: Did you notice we focus completely on Bible, along with math, phonics and handwriting? Go to the library and load up on books. Snuggle on the couch. Get outside. These are ample for this age group.

The Habit of Morning Room Time – How Mama Can Be in Two Places at One Time

The question I heard most often when our eldest was just a little more than a year old: "What about the little ones?" It's also the question the Lord used to work on my heart about homeschooling.

If the Lord is tugging on your heart too about homeschooling, I can offer encouragement. I understand the need to have just a small span of time to focus on something other than your preschooler. That needed time could be teaching and working with your older children. Or it might simply be that you are in survival mode and needing to breathe or get a shower.

See, I knew I wanted to keep my child home with me. She learned so easily at home, was very bright and loved books. A close friend suggested an answer. She told me about morning room time.

Morning room time is the best, overall answer for so many of the challenges with little ones. It's how I can practice ABCs with my little one, sing the B-I-B-L-E *and* help my older children with math – all at the same time. My husband and I made a recording of these basic songs and more. We recorded both my husband's voice and mine – for our child to listen to for anywhere from 10 and up to 40 minutes. What's included?

- Practice time learning our address

- Polite manners we want our children to exemplify in Sunday church services
- Bible verses to memorize
- Fun nursery rhyme songs

A simple script is available in the book *Creative Family Times* (see Favorite Resources).

Morning room time is a habit built with practice. Your smallest ones can listen to your recording for five to 10 minutes in the crib while watching a mobile. Slowly add longer time over the course of days and weeks.

During morning time, toddlers can stack blocks, thumb through books, play with a few favorite toys just designated for room time. This small amount of time is a gift not only to the parent and older siblings but a gift to the child practicing room time. A small amount of alone time, playing independently, gives the child time to build small motor skills working puzzles. No one else is showing him how to stack blocks or line up small figures in a line. He is working on that independently. Do you see the beauty? The overall benefits for the whole family?

Morning Room Time is the habit that blesses all ages. As my children have grown, I see so many other skills they have that stem from the morning room time habit.

Meanwhile, during morning time, the older children are starting their basics: math, English, spelling, handwriting. I am able to help the older three get started, help with questions and more. All because of morning room time.

My children have all outgrown morning room time now but I continue to see the benefits. And they still wander off about mid-morning, for just a bit of a quiet break. They find something to do. That habit is a result of tested and proven morning room time.

> **Hodgepodge Hint:** Morning room time made it possible for me to have time to teach older children – especially math – through five babies and years of homeschooling so far. It's a tried and true habit.

How Morning Room Time Builds Learning Skills for Later

Fast forward a few years. Now, when I am teaching and helping the older children, the younger children entertain themselves. They play with each other. Or they play independently. They do not follow me around and ask for me to entertain them. All those mornings they were younger and practicing this habit, it wasn't just play time. It was skill building.

I am not saying that it is all rosy posy pudding and pie in our home all the time. We have our moments. We have our training times. But I found myself sitting and schooling with one of the older children and wondering where the youngest was. If I listened for a minute I could hear him off in the other room playing with trains.

During family studies after lunch, I am again thankful for the skill building of morning room time. The younger two enjoy drawing at the kitchen table while I read. So I ask them to stay and listen. But then one will ask to get down from the table. Rather than departing altogether, that child more often than not will play close by. And he will continue to listen.

After five children participating in morning room time, I continue to see the benefits:

- Increased concentration
- Extended attention span
- Listening while playing
- Development of small motor skills
- A love of music
- Playing independently

The Lord Will Equip You

If the Lord has placed that desire in you to homeschool your children, He will equip and encourage you. This Morning Room Time Habit is exactly what He provided for us. Building this habit, in small time increments and practicing habits isn't always easy. But I encourage you to stick with it! That Morning Room Time is a gift to your child.

> *Haven't I commanded you? Strength! Courage! Don't be timid; don't get discouraged. God, your God, is with you every step you take.* Joshua 1:9

Hodgepodge Hint: Are you lamenting the absence of a preschool experience? Yes, your child might not make handprint paintings with a room full of other preschoolers. But you can give your child opportunity for artistic times with all of your children. Plan some special preschool learning times.

The Habit of One More Thing After Lunch

This is the *one thing* **that really changed my attitude.** When the children were all little we could usually get most of our learning completed before lunch. As they grew and the needs of the age range grew as well, I struggled to fit it all. My friend, Kerri, chimed in with, "we do one more thing after lunch." That concept, that **one** schedule change, revolutionized our thinking.

In the morning we have our morning room time, we complete our three Rs, piano practice and a few other things. **Then during – and right after – lunch we spend time on one or more subjects.** History, science, vocabulary, or composer and artist study. Following is a list we choose from each day. We have typical days for certain ones so I am prepared with supplies we might need.

Each day / One or more of the following:

- History
- Science
- Vocabulary
- Composers and artists
- Latin
- Art or hands on activity
- Nature study
- Biology lesson for the older ones

Do you see how this habit helps us to accomplish quite a bit during a week? How it helps a mama to not feel quite so overwhelmed? The learning is spaced out over an entire week. And there is time to enjoy. Plus the children don't mind just 'one more thing' after lunch. We found that as the children grew older, this habit grew into several more things after lunch.

All of this learning *everyone* **participates in.** Sometimes I read aloud while they eat their lunch. Now, the younger children might hop down from the kitchen table after they are finished eating. But they've already caught the meat of the lesson. Because they were right there eating while I was reading. For foreign language studies, we move to the adjoining family room and plop on the couches. Younger ones play close by, build with the blocks. But you'd be surprised how much they enjoy any additional lessons too!

One More Subject After Lunch has changed our lives and added the spice to our lasagna learning!

Hodgepodge Hint: I have our supplies close to the kitchen table – in our Most Used Bookshelf. The Most Used Bookshelf is an IKEA 2x4 bookcase with cubbies and baskets. Maybe you have a rolling cart? I keep our most used items in the Most Used Bookshelf because I know we'll need the resources right when we are all gathered at the kitchen table. It's less prep when we do our learning all together. Imagine if I had to prepare each of these subjects times five children!

How to Fit in All the Homeschool Extras

There just might be some of us pulling along a big bag of guilt for not getting to certain things in our homeschool. Do you have curriculum still sitting on your shelf – yet to crack it open? It's okay. There are so many circumstances keeping us from enjoying the extras.

How to fit in the extras is one of the most frequently asked questions I've received as a homeschool mama. Here are some strategies to help you with those homeschool extras. Even if you are cruising along pretty well. But, first off…

What are the homeschool extras? And are they really extras?

Well, in our house we call them the extras because they are the *really fun part* of homeschooling. The icing on the homeschool cake. The things we look forward to. But I feel strongly that mixing in a balance of enriching subjects makes for a happy child and a happy mama. A well-educated child.

My definition of extras is any other subject. Yes, science and history are essential around third grade and up, but in our home, we work those around the basic subjects. Take a glance at what the Hodgepodge homeschool defines as the extras:

- Science, nature study
- History
- Geography
- Writing and composition skills
- Etiquette

- Foreign language
- Computer skills, programming
- Life skills
- PE
- Extracurricular activities such as drama troupe
- Music lessons
- Fine arts
- Art!
- Robotics
- Photography
- Ham radio licensing

Fitting in the enriching homeschool extras can work in several ways.

Hodgepodge Hint: One way we fit in homeschool extras is to do the learning together. All the ages, all the children studying one or more subjects – matching each child's age and ability.

The Habit of Time Management

Time is on your side, homeschool friends. It really is. You really aren't behind. You really *can* enjoy the extras. Here I share my best tips for time management. You may be aware of some of these helpful habits. But you may be like me and need a reminder. Those days I feel stressed and wonder how we are going to fit it all in…when we are being stretched thin…

These are the habits that have blessed our homeschool and opened wide the doors to more! These simple steps I've found are key to fitting in the extras for us. First…

Start Earlier

But how? I'll admit I am a morning person. But my teens are not. So we have a little give and take there. Often I can start the day with the little ones while my upper grade children are still getting breakfast. This works. By the time the youngest ones are done and can play together, I am available for the older ones.

Act Like Homeschoolers

You'd think that this would come naturally for me but it didn't. I was raised in a public school setting and really had to coach myself on schooling at other times besides 8-3. We can act like homeschoolers! A few ideas for fitting in subjects in the homeschool way:

- Do read alouds at bedtime
- Listen to audio books in the car when you are going to and fro

- Focus on more difficult subjects in the evenings when a child needs a little help from Dad
- Complete science labs on the weekend a.k.a. Science Saturdays
- Spend time reading during afternoon quiet time

One More Thing After Lunch

One more thing after lunch. As mentioned in an earlier chapter, this is a simple way to assure time for a subject. As children grow into the high school years, lunch is a natural break before an afternoon of history, science and other subjects.

Our Schedule for Extras

We sort of have certain days of the week we enjoy the extras. **But it's very flexible.** Sometimes we rotate. Sometimes we do a little more. While the children eat lunch, I often read aloud. Sometimes I go ahead and read aloud our science lesson for the day.

Here is an example of our schedule for extras:

- Monday – nature study with science (though they aren't limited to that day. Older ones continue science daily.)
- Tuesday – science and/or history, foreign language, root word study
- Wednesday – art and composer study
- Thursday – history, foreign language, root word study, science
- Friday – history arts and activities

Group the Extracurricular Together

My children are involved in just enough extracurricular activities to keep me from being stressed out. And, it took me a while, but I learned to group those things together on the same days. One day we have piano lessons and choir activities. Another day we have drama troupe practice. I often schedule appointments around the same time I know we will be out.

This gives me a guarantee. I know that I will be home at least two and often three full days a week. The whole day to accomplish learning. That is so very important for getting school work accomplished. And being home is important for fitting in all the extras!

Hodgepodge Hint: A useful exercise might be to write out all the extras and extracurricular activities your family plans to tackle. Prioritize, mix and match and fit them into certain days.

The Homeschool Extras Within Sight

Now friends, this tip is one that was just right there in front of my face. Right within sight. A couple of years ago, when trying to find an answer for the overflowing library book basket, I looked up and spied the mantel. I thought, why not? I set aside the usual thoughts of what a mantel was 'supposed' to look. And I arranged those homeschool books right there. Right within sight. Made practical use of the central focus of the family room.

Guess what? I've found we get much more homeschooling done in a day simply because we can see the books. Because the resources are within easy reach. We fit that extra learning into our day.

But that's not all. We have books on the end tables. They prop the lamps. Even the extra books that are for pure pleasure – not really part of any curriculum – are stacked where my children can see them.

This keeping homeschool resources within sight is a bit of a passion for me. It's an ongoing homeschool makeover to meet the needs of our homeschool, our children.

Here are a few more ideas:

- Bible Basket – many Bibles right in the middle of the family room table
- The Word Within Sight – framed scripture on the walls and on the doorposts of the house
- History Shelf - IKEA bookshelf makes it handy for history books, lapbooks and more
- Most Used Bookshelf – right beside the kitchen table where we can reach the extras
- Chalkboard Desk – handy for writing letters, for math problems and creating roadways for toy cars
- Maps as Window Treatments – geography within sight
- Preschool to 1st grade Organization – learning areas include a little bench, desks and a spot for mama!

To top it all off, a magazine rack sits right above our family room couch. The rack houses the newest choice for our science study, our individual, daily planners…all those extras we want to fit in our day!

There's a lot to this homeschooling life, isn't there? I've found that keeping things within sight – in an organized sort of manner, sure helps this mama.

Hodgepodge Hint: I share these habits so you might take one thing for inspiration. One rearrangement that might work. Just remember that all of these areas were created and put in place over the course of several years.

Declare An Extras Day!

In more ways than one, clearing my calendar can be freeing. There's just something wonderful about a long stretch of time without commitments. Children feel the same way when they aren't hurried through activities. A whole day to paint and create? *Yes, please.*

Knowing that I can give our homeschool an 'extras' day was somewhat revolutionary to me. Why? Because all of sudden a couple of weeks fly by and we still haven't read the rest of that book or we still haven't made a salt dough map. Or it's rained and we haven't taken a nature walk in what seems like ages.

So, every now and then I just declare a full day of extras. Truth be told these are the biggest memory making days of all. Sure there are messes but we're already pulling out this and that for a history project, so why not do an art lesson? Indeed why not? We are homeschoolers.

When? You could set aside one Friday a month for an extras day. You could do all the extras one day a week even! Or, as I shared in my Time Management section, you can do one extra each day of the week. There's just something about making a day of it. Here are a few examples of Extra Days we enjoy:

Hands on Geography

Yes, if all your ages are included then you get all those sensory and motor skills practice in for the youngest ones. Making a salt dough map – reading a recipe. Make it art by painting the continents.

Art Afternoons

While this isn't usually a whole day, I often figure that while we have all the art supplies out for history, we might as well enjoy a few art lessons and pull out the chalk pastels too.

History Days

We sit by the fire and read and read and read. Some children work on history notebooks while I read. Another child puts together a display board. Someone could even write an outline for a book report.

Immersing your children in a full day of extras will help them to see all the fun of that particular subject. It will also help you feel accomplished as the parent/teacher and set aside any guilt of not fitting certain things in.

I hope with these ideas you have been encouraged to enjoy these enriching subjects in your homeschool.

Hodgepodge Hints:

-Sometimes it simply takes an adjustment in thinking on your part as the parent. Sometimes it's a schedule change. Just pick the one 'extra' that appeals to you and your children the most. First, do those three Rs well, and then fit in the fun!

As your children reach the high school years, a fun way to fit in the extras is to do night school. Gather around, make some hot chocolate, and enjoy a subject together.

The Habit of Afternoon Quiet Time

So I've been sharing the learning layers of our homeschool day. First, we place a generous helping of prayer, next we layer all those helpful homeschool habits, we stir around the 3 Rs on five levels. After lunch we sprinkle the wonderful spices of enrichment, showing how we fit in all the extra Hodgepodge of learning. So now…

Are you ready to put your feet up and relax? I am! Afternoon quiet time is the longest running habit for us. The afternoon quiet time layer gives a spot of quiet for all ages. Back when my first toddler outgrew her nap I wondered what to do. See, I needed that time. Why did she outgrow her nap when I had an infant to take care of too? Afternoon quiet time was the answer.

When our eldest outgrew her nap I struggled with losing that quiet time for myself. I *needed* it! The three-month-old was napping. I also noticed she and I were both able to handle late afternoons better when we had our afternoon quiet time. Since those early days, the lines blur as to just how quiet time came about in our home.

However it came to be, quiet time is just that. Quiet. Everybody in their own spot. Separate and away. Each afternoon the baby naps and the rest are (ideally) quiet.

The Afternoon Quiet Time rules: Everyone gathers what they need. Each one goes to a bedroom or other area of the house away from everyone else. No coming out of your room for that pair of scissors you forgot or a for a new coloring book. No calling Mama. No computer. No TV. Put things back when quiet time is over. Then, enjoy having a bit of quiet in a blessed, busy household!

Children can:

- Read books
- Listen to the radio
- Listen to an audio book (lots at the library!)
- Color, work on an art project
- Use their imagination – play quietly with anything in the room
- Write a letter, add to a journal

To start out reluctant quiet-timers, we focused on the child's current favorite. Our eldest boy loved nature field guides. As an emerging reader, he would sit for as long as an adult would and listen to details on birds, insects, etc. My mother borrowed a few of the guides and recorded her reading them aloud for him. For his quiet time he would gather his stack of guides and turn on the day's topic. See how the learning continues independently? See how habits are growing?

Mom gets quiet time too! Yes you can catch up on household chores **but make sure you allow yourself at least 15 minutes of something enjoyable.** Have a cup of coffee, catch up on emails (mom is allowed computer time), prop your feet up.

Afternoon Quiet Time can also created some freedoms. It can be a time when:

- youngest reader sits near Mama and practices reading with the favorite readers or books
- older child can have much needed one on one time with Mama
- opportunity comes for a nature study by the window
- catch up on a report or project
- practice lines for drama troupe

When quiet time is over it is tea time and/or outside time. Since everyone has been apart for a while, usually siblings get along better and are so ready to play! Soon you'll be finding yourself saying, "Ahhh... It's quiet time."

Hodgepodge Hints:

- As children grow older, Afternoon Quiet Time becomes a natural space in the day for renewal. Ideally this time does not include screen time. That habit comes later in the day.
- Know that in a perfect world all children obey and are quiet for the designated time. Be prepared for training moments. Also know that, as with any new habit, it takes practice. Just like my hints for creating a successful morning room time, you may want to start with a shorter time and work up to the amount of time you desire. Build the time in increment then celebrate even small successes with tea time!

Afternoon Quiet Time Tips

Guess what? During holiday or summer time, as we leave the morning schedule of school work, afternoon quiet time becomes our anchor. It's the structure of the day that is always there. Even when summer refreshingly changes up our days with outside activities and other opportunities. And especially when holiday activities pack the calendar.

- **How long should quiet time last?** If you don't have an established afternoon quiet time, start small. Fifteen minutes at a time and building up. Be patient as your children get used to this time. Be especially with a child dropping a nap. I usually have a child getting used to quiet time in the same room with me so that I can model the habit. Audio books really, really help! Our Quiet Times last anywhere from half an hour to two hours *depending on the day and our needs*. Rarely do our Quiet Times go two hours. Often I will reward those who have done as they have been asked by allowing them come out early and play quietly together.

- **My children share a bedroom. How can we do separate afternoon quiet times?** We have two sisters and two brothers sharing rooms at our house. So, we designate quiet times in other areas of the house. One child has quiet time in the dining room turned music room. Another may set up a spot in a quiet corner near a bookcase. Yet another might just sit close by on the couch with me. Often we rotate quiet time spots to keep things fresh and to take turns with the bedrooms. We even have quiet time outside. Be creative!

- **I have two very active children who don't like to be alone. How do I make Afternoon Quiet Time work?** Know ahead of time it will be tough. That's the biggest part for me. Even though this is a habit in our home, often I have to reign this afternoon time back in.

This is when I know I might need to:

1. Keep one child close to me for guidance for several afternoons.
2. Borrow some new audio books from the library. Just like school time, afternoon quiet time takes planning too! But not much more than just reserving some extra fun at the library.
3. Let the children know that quiet time is over when the recording or audio book is over. That takes the time limit off of you. And cuts down on the "Is Quiet Time over yet?" questions.
4. Assign a project. Make sure all the supplies are gathered prior to Quiet Time so there is no asking for scissors and tape.
5. Let my crafty child pull out those art kits she received as gifts.
6. Dedicate this hour or more to uninterrupted building time for my blocks and bricks lover.

I hope this gives you some ideas of the blessing Afternoon Quiet Time can be in your home. The investment in building the habit is worth it for years to come.

Hodgepodge Hint: Quiet Time can be a built in time of day to say yes to many of the things your child can do quietly on his or her own.

The Habit of Afternoon Quiet Time for Mama

"Honey, take a nap."

Some of the best advice my grandmother ever gave me. Yes, young children need a nap. But did you know that mothers need one too?

"You just need to put your feet up for 10 minutes. Even if you don't go to sleep. As long as you relax for 10 to 15 minutes, you'll be able to face the crazy hours."

So I have taken my grandmother's advice ever since I became a mama. As much as I can.

Now, with children in the house, your quiet time habit must be established. Yes! Before embarking on the habit of napping, my five are in their own quiet time spots. (See the Habit of Afternoon Quiet Time)

Once children are secured in their Afternoon Quiet Time Routine:

- Find a comfortable spot
- Put your feet up
- Put your head back
- Close your eyes
- And relax
- *Really.* **Relax**
- Just 10-15 minutes

I am convinced that the world would be a better place if we'd all just take an afternoon nap. Close to supper time, tempers would flare less. Stress would more easily be diffused. All because Mama took a nap. "Ooo weee, girl. I can tell you didn't get your nap today!"

That's my prescription. *The Habit of Napping.*

I encourage you. Establish quiet time. Then take a nap a day.

> **Hodgepodge Hint:** Don't fret. The laundry *will still be there*. Trust me. You will get to fix supper for your crew. Relax first. Quiet Time and an afternoon nap will give you the ammunition you need to accomplish those necessary tasks.

The Habit of Celebrating

The incredible gift of the ordinary! Glory comes streaming from the table of daily life. ~ Macrina Wiederkehr

Before you even begin to shape (or re-shape!) your homeschool life, schedule or environment, why not adopt the habit of celebrating *every* day? Celebrate a lost tooth, an extra measure of kindness, diligence in school work or finding the long-lost library book.

At first the special plate was only pulled out for birthdays. But then I read this celebratory idea and love it.

Several times during the week someone gets the special plate. Often we rotate through the family based on age. Even Mama and Daddy get a turn!

Whoever has the special plate at supper time gets to lead us in the blessing. Then at some point during the meal, when tummies are about full, we ask the question. "What do you appreciate about (whoever has the plate that day)?"

I made a mental list of what everyone shared about the six-year-old the other night. One said, "I appreciate her because she plays great Barbie stories." Another exclaimed, "I like how she plays outside with me and bird watches with me." Daddy said, "I appreciate how she's made an extra effort to keep her room clean this week!" The three-year-old said, "I appreciate her because she is a sweet sister."

Honestly, sometimes this time helps us work through some hurt feelings from earlier in the day. This time of celebrating gets us talking. The gratitude gets us focusing on the good. Plus, practicing gratitude daily helps build the habit of gratitude.

Any plate will do. Maybe you don't have a red "You are special today" plate but another pretty one to recognize the special person of the day. And it doesn't have to be reserved for the evening meal. Next pretty day, have a tea party!

The point is to find reasons to celebrate the every day. Use it. Let it get chipped on the sides from overuse.

Hodgepodge Hint: Using the You Are Special Today plate is really just a practical way we can encourage each other and practice Ephesians 4:29: *Let no corrupt communication proceed out of your mouth, but that which is good to use in edifying, that it may minister grace unto the hearers.*

The Habit of Communication

Mad sad glad is a little game we play at supper time once or twice a week. It's a gem I learned from Drs. Les and Leslie Parrott's Parenting the Early Years.

It's as the name says. You take turns as you go around the table. Everyone takes turns and shares what made them mad, sad and glad that day. Let's face it. We all can think of something for each category – little ones, older children, even us adults.

Honestly, this helps us get beyond the sit down, chew with your mouth closed, lean over and eat your peas commands. The game also gets everyone talking, allowing us parents to help the children to work through some emotions we each face daily. We might even remember something we'd already dismissed in our minds.

Sometimes the children ask to play mad sad glad as we are riding in the car or tucking in at bedtime. It's a good opener for all kinds of discussion. Maybe there was something awful that happened in the news. There will be failures. People will disappoint us. We want to educate them on how to handle something hard. Why does so and so happen? Well, ultimately because there is sin in this imperfect world. Yet we can find comfort in the fact that God has the whole world in His hands.

So, the mad sad glad game has served us well. It helps us to slow down and talk at suppertime. Gives us a chance to work through situations. And it is always good to end with the glad.

The Habit of Enjoying
The Great Freedoms of Homeschooling

There are too many freedoms with homeschooling to count. However, here are several favorites to get you going and encourage you along the way.

Great Freedom #1 Continuing education for mama! For example, I am gaining an understanding of the history timeline that I never grasped in my years of school.

Great Freedom #2 An incredible expansion of time management skills. A constant tweaking of habits to adjust for ages and stages.

Great Freedom #3 Plenty of outside time! There time in the day to cultivate curiosity with nature study and explore in your own yard.

Great Freedom #4 Time to get sidetracked now and then. Sometimes getting sidetracked is a good thing! When a millipede interrupts math you just might have to open the front door to put it back outside. Capturing the millipede, gently in a paper cup, of course prompts an older brother to share a comparison list of millipedes vs. centipedes he recently learned from his high school Biology text. Opening the door might cause two boys to notice a slug…

Great Freedom #5 You can adjust the day towards relationships with immediate and extended family members. You can finish up school work for the day and go visit with a grandparent. Better yet, load up the books and lunch and move school to great-grandparent's backyard!

Great Freedom #6 Sleep comes easily at night for Mama – days are full, challenging and rewarding. I tend to be worn out and sleep well each night!

Great Freedom #7 You can say yes often! Yes you can mop the floor. Yes you can wear a 'thinking cap' for school. Yes, pick out as many books as you like at the library and then pile up on the couch.

Great Freedom #8 A total turn about in decorating and organization, i.e. – The Homeschool Makeover. Our learning is all over the house. We are always moving things around and improving. We of course haven't ever had a dining room but we do have a music room for piano practice and more. We've also just recently added desks on each end of the very narrow closet in the girls' bedroom. They each have their own space.

Great Freedom #9 Tailoring an education for each and every one of our children. Hitting directly the needs, the learning styles as well as the fun of chasing an answer when we want to!

Great Freedom #10 Building relationships with our children and all things of eternal value.

The Habit of Singing

We all have those moments. The overwhelming, frustrating time of wanting to yell or scream at the top of our lungs. Well, I've found one way of diverting the irritating. When you want to scream, just sing. Turn it to praise!

For example, when everything is spread far and wide after a morning of homeschooling, you can pull a line from a favorite song or hymn. A beautiful voice is not required. Just an attitude of gratitude to slice through the overwhelm.

Praise God from Whom All Blessings Flow! Praise Him All Creatures Here Below…Praise Him Above Ye Heavenly Host. Praise Father, Son and Holy Ghost. Amen!!

Here are a few more to sing out:

"God bless America! Land that I love!"

"Jesus, Jesus, Jesus; There's just something about that name! Master, Savior, Jesus, Like the fragrance after the rain…"

"O the King is coming, the King is coming! I just heard the trumpets sounding, And now His face I see…"

And do you know will happen? The frustration will turn to laughter! Sometimes we all dissolve into silly laughter. And it is so good for the soul.

"Come on, let's clean this up," I was able to say in a calm voice. And it truly didn't take long to get all those school books rounded up. The time it took to turn that frustration into song? Less time than the clean up.

> *...in everything give thanks; for this is God's will for you in Christ Jesus.* 1 Thessalonians 5:18

The Habit of Stepping Outside

Sometimes when it's been a full day. I step outside.

Just for a minute.

And I take it in.

The hydrangeas by the front door. A day lily on its last bit of bloom.

I walk around to the back. Unhook the latch, step through the gate. The garden is there. Needing a weed pulled.

I look up. See a sliver of moon. A puff of a cloud. The sunset reflected in purple and orange.

By now I'm to the back door. I quietly swing it open and step back in.

Just a short walk outside, around the house. A breath of fresh air. A new perspective.

And a better wife, better mama for it. Refreshed to freely love. Ready to tuck in precious ones. Listen to prayers. Be thankful.

> *The best things are nearest…light in your eyes, flowers at your feet, duties at your hand, the path of God just before you.* ~Robert Louis Stevenson

The Habit of Catching Up

We are usually finished with our school year by the first week of May each year. That's because we start homeschool the last week of July. We choose to do this so that we can have the freedom to take off when we'd like to, refocus our December learning, *and* so we have built in time for just such a year of challenges.

There are homeschooling years that will be different. We've had years with months of sickness, procedures and sidetracks. Despite all that, we *are successful*. We *have learned*.

Here is a plan you can use to catch up. You truly aren't behind. You are just about where we need to be. You just need to refocus and work to rearrange and fit in those lovely subjects you let go when schedules got crazy.

Hodgepodge Remedy for Catch Up

Be positive and focus on all that you have already accomplished! I've found that I spin my wheels if I focus on all we need to get done or all we haven't done. However, if I list the successes, I am encouraged.

Have a Plan But Be Flexible

Take a look at the calendar for the week. Ask your children for their input on catching up and having a different sort of schedule to complete assignments.

Get Up Early

Yes, we are homeschoolers but we can get up early. It gives us more time to catch up! Starting 30-60 minutes earlier can make all the difference between staying behind and catching up.

Triage Assignments

Determine what needs the most focus – from all those things clamoring for your attention. Start with a list of all that needs to get done. Hit the urgent. Save the others for another week.

Make an Afternoon of It

Get your basic subjects completed in the morning. Then spend an entire afternoon on a subject you need to catch up on. You and your students can devote entire afternoons to one subject while making sure you are still covering all those basics you need to do every day.

Just Do It

Even if it goes into the evening. Even if it takes the whole day. Better to do it now because those spring days are coming and the fresh air and sunshine will be calling to you!

Celebrate!

Head to the park, pull out the paints, make cookies. You've worked hard and are on the road to catching up. Time to celebrate!

> *The Lord will work out His plans for my life – for your faithful love, O Lord, endures forever.* Psalm 138:8

Hodgepodge Hint: When we have a few sick I declare a reading afternoon. Everyone get comfy, rest and read!

The Habit of Homeschooling in December

I invite you to come and sit by the fire, enjoy a warm cup of coffee, hot chocolate or tea and put your feet up – *for about five minutes.* Just five minutes because in December things are changing moment to moment. Like most families, it's so very busy. Time to head to this practice, get your dress shoes for this performance and, *oh dear, another child with a fever.* Precisely why…

We take December off from homeschool. Well, in reality we don't completely take the month off. We just change up our learning.

It's simply a new twist on subjects. Baking Christmas cookies becomes math, decorating and writing thank you notes count for handwriting. We are so blessedly busy with all kinds of drama troupe productions, choir programs, piano recitals and more!

Family read aloud – Each year we pick a favorite, family read aloud for advent. This is a most anticipated time!

Worship with choirs at Church – all those wonderful hymns, children's choirs help us focus on the true meaning of the Christmas season.

Piano – A recital coming up makes Christmas music fill the house.

Drama Troupe – Christmas performances take up a good portion of time in December. So we purposefully leave open space and down time around practice times.

Living Math – Baking cookies – our favorite recipe for measuring, adding and counting

Handwriting – Thank you notes, addressing Christmas cards.

Unstructured Art – Painting those thank you notes, making homemade Hodgepodge wrapping paper, making gifts like a painted canvas.

Reading for Pleasure – Often an annual favorite like The Best Christmas Pageant Ever.

Nature Study – we do a 'hunt for red and green' on a nature walk this time of year. Amazing how much we notice so many other colors in nature.

Hodgepodge Hint: Our focus is on all the celebratory things leading up to Christmas. And it looks a little different each year according to ages and stages. So, it's a Hodgepodge of homeschooling in December.

The Habits of Housekeeping

About twice a year I find myself smack dab in the middle of the habit of purging. Since I find myself in the overwhelm of this task, I thought there might be some of you doing the same – and feeling the overwhelm too? These housekeeping habits not only help with clutter busting, they are basic. The ones that rescue me when I'm surrounded. The ones that even bless children.

These are the habits – with rewards – we turn to *daily*. Yes, we've tried other housekeeping, picking up and cleaning up strategies. But these are the ones that stick for *us*. What is expected by everyone. So here is *what has worked for years:*

As with every habit, take it at your speed. Pick what will bless your life. Just a few minutes can make the difference in how the house looks. It can also do wonders for mama's attitude.

So, once again, I find myself having a little pep talk. "A little five minute pick up and this place will be spiffed up. Then I won't want to put my head down and cry."

Habits and Routines

When I get overwhelmed with housework, I fall back on Flylady habits (see Favorite Resources section). Her basic tools have helped me get going in the morning, tackle laundry, take care of myself and teach the children to help pick up. Teaching children to do these type of household tasks is an important life skill.

Jurisdictions

"Time to pick up jurisdictions," I call.

There is honestly no way I could possibly follow behind five children and keep our home straight. *And* homeschool. Since we are all part of a family, all should contribute. Carving the big job into smaller parts makes it easier for everyone. We adopted the jurisdiction habit from the famed Duggar family.

> **Jurisdiction**: the territory or sphere of activity over which the legal authority of a court or other institution extends.

Simply translated for our home, a jurisdiction is the area a child is responsible for maintaining. Pick up the toys, keep the area clean. To start with, each child is responsible for his or her own bedroom. Those that share a room share in the duty.

But each child is also in charge of another area of the house. Older ones have a bit more responsibility. Here's a peek at the way our jurisdiction lines are drawn:

- Eldest girl: bedroom, upstairs shared bath, classroom
- Eldest boy: shared bedroom, downstairs shared bath, family room, his quiet time space
- Middle girl: shared bedroom, music room (her quiet time spot)
- Youngest girl: shared bedroom, her quiet time space
- Youngest boy: putting toys back in bucket after room time

We take time to pick up jurisdictions several times a day: before lunch, after Afternoon Quiet Time and before bedtime. A tidy jurisdiction is a prerequisite for a 4 pm screen time turn. Usually all that is needed is a five minute room rescue. Make it a game – set the timer and see if you can beat it.

So what happens when someone makes a mess in someone else's jurisdiction? Either the two share in the work or the one in charge of that area cleans it up. We've found this to be an important lesson. Having charge of an area promotes responsibility *and* is a learning opportunity. When a mess is made *somebody* has to clean it up. Isn't that true all the way through life?

Hodgepodge Hint: Jurisdictions are the basic duties. From there we add in those tasks I am willing to pay for.

The Habit of Service Opportunities

Which sounds better to you – a household task or a chance to help? When I think of *chore* I think of Eeyore, hanging his head down because he has to rebuild his house of sticks, *again*.

However, in *service*, we can choose to find freedom. Service is a choice.

> *It is absolutely clear that God has called you to a free life. Just make sure that you don't use this freedom as an excuse to do whatever you want to do and destroy your freedom. Rather, use your freedom to serve one another in love; that's how freedom grows. For everything we know about God's Word is summed up in a single sentence: Love others as you love yourself. That's an act of true freedom…*Galatians 5:13

In our home, we have basic expectations for everyone. Make your bed. Pick up after yourself. Clear your spot at the table. Maintain your jurisdiction. However, most things above and beyond the basics we will gladly PAY to be done. Paid jobs are called service opportunities. This is an idea we have adapted from Doorposts (please see Resources section).

Home Blessing Hour. One fun way the children can earn quick service opportunities money is during our weekly home blessing hour. We put jobs on strips of paper and each draws one. The timer is set for 10 minutes.

When the timer beeps, run and choose a new opportunity. Youngest children can tag along with Mama or an older sibling. Having a buddy especially works well with emptying trash.

Reluctant helper? Whiner? Arguer? With service opportunities there is a built in reward for cheerfulness and a happy spirit. *Double pay* is disbursed if the task is performed without complaining and arguing. In our home, the basic home blessing tasks just listed pay 25 cents each. But if the service is finished with a happy spirit, the pay is 50 cents.

Other service opportunities we regularly reward include but are not limited to:

- Bug removal (thank you Lord, for my brave boys)
- Laundry (carrying clothes from the dirty clothes hamper to laundry room)
- Kitchen (set table, help cook, fill drink cups)
- Dishes (rinsing, loading/unloading dishwasher)
- Bringing in firewood
- Getting mail/delivering mail to box
- Help with young ones (changing/fetching a diaper)
- Weeding/yard work (extra $)
- Cleaning out the family van (pay extra for a good cleaning!)
- Cleaning the bathroom (a separate payment each for cleaning the toilet, tub, sink)
- Groceries (bringing in and putting away groceries)

Every good and perfect gift is from above, and comes down from the Father of lights, with whom there is no variation or shadow of turning. James 1:17

Hopefully, by teaching our children to serve in the home, they will take advantage of service opportunities outside the home. Their hearts will be tuned to recognize an area they are skilled to serve or simply a way to bless another. And when these children grow up in just a short while, their employers and coworkers can confidently entrust them with opportunities, reward them for a job well done.

Hodgepodge Hint: Take good care. Service opportunities teach another important character trait – caring for the gifts we've been given.

The Habit of Rewarding Service

By Hodgepodgedad

As parents, we want our children to have wisdom, faithfulness, and diligence. They need to be able to handle money wisely. They also need to learn how to work. We combine these two goals; we pay our children for a portion of their work around the house. The Bible clearly links work with material gain. It also links work to our very sustenance (see 2 Thes. 3:10-12).

God does not give allowances to those who won't work (although He does provide for those who can't). We are living in a time when some believe that they are "entitled" to something for which they did not work.

"What do your children do with all of that money?" you may ask. We divide earnings into seven categories:

- Charity
- Tithe
- Living expenses
- Discretionary spending
- Short-term savings
- Long-term savings
- Dowry

Each category has a portion of the child's earnings assigned. A spreadsheet allows us to quickly calculate the amount going to each category by entering the number of Service Opportunities completed during the previous week.

Spending money is given to each child. Savings (the last three categories) are spirited away to a savings account. Tithe and charity money is placed into an envelope to give away.

Our children now earn their spending money, understand that God expects faithfulness in giving, and know that they have money saved for a "rainy day".

Hodgepodge Hint: The folks at Doorposts have a publication that explains the concept in detail (complete with bible verses to help you instruct your children). It is called *Stewardship Street, A Road to Financial Faithfulness* (see Resource section). It was our guide as we started teaching our children about how to handle work and money.

The Hodgepodge Homeschooling Method

Our homeschooling method is one that came about over time. Would it surprise you to know that our methods truly are a hodgepodge? One ingredient added. Another sifted in. Mixing slowly. Seasoning to taste.

The roots of our homeschooling method are classical. There's a healthy dose of Charlotte Mason enrichment. Plus, the unit studies help us all learn together. And the whole-hearted approach speaks of each child's relationship with the Lord. *Please see the appendix for more information on homeschooling methods and learning styles.

So, in no particular order, here are the top 10 the reasons this Hodgepodge method works for us:

1. **The fun factor.** Mixing up several styles adds variety to an education.
2. **Learning styles.** Using a mix of homeschool methods and approaches helps the auditory, kinesthetic, visual and independent student learn.
3. **Varying Age levels.** Meeting the ever-changing learning opportunities as the children grow.
4. **Charlotte Mason.** We've found this education method added the wonderful, joyful aspects we didn't even know were lacking in our homeschool. Nature studies. Art and music appreciation. Notebooking, journaling, writing. It has all opened our eyes and helped us appreciate. Charlotte Mason also speaks highly of habits.
5. **Habits are definitely the bones of our day.** Habits help us 'fit it all in' and get food on the table.

Habits give us a comfortable framework. Habits help the children know what to expect.

7. **Living Books.** Rick and glorious reading. Classic books we learn from, soak up and enjoy!

8. **Classical covers it.** "The heart of a classical education lies in the trivium – the grammar, logic and rhetoric stages. These coincide with natural learning abilities during childhood. For most families, classical education includes a dedication to in-depth studies of Latin, mathematics, the arts and sciences, and a deep understanding of world history and its effects that lure them in. Many classical homeschoolers follow a four-year or six-year cycle of repeating science and history topics." – The Curriculum Choice.

9. **Biblical Principle Approach/Biblical Worldview.** We see the world through our creation-based glasses. We turn to the Bible for answers since it is the authority in our lives as well as our first history and science book.

10. **Whole-Hearted Learning.** With many living books at the offering and the heart as the key to all learning.

11. **Relaxed, Delight-Directed.** Very few textbooks or workbooks. We leave room for this each day with our one more thing after lunch and afternoon quiet time habits. We love our delight-directed art time. Reading books for pleasure. Building time with blocks. We also enjoy simply running, swinging and playing outside in the backyard.

Hodgepodge Hint: Homeschool methods meet individual learning needs well.

10 Parts of the Hodgepodge Homeschool Schedule

Our homeschool day doesn't always happen exactly like this. Sometimes the lines blur. And there are daily challenges. But these are the basic bones, the habits of our day:

1. Before 8:45

   Bible and morning quiet time are included. As well as all the regular sorts of reminders like brushing teeth, making your bed, clearing your spot at the breakfast table and even getting dressed. Rest assured there are those days it is more like a *Before 9:45*.

2. Little ones first

   Sometimes we might start the day with a 'circle time' all together. But always, before I oversee the older ones I first help the littlest ones with their math, phonics and handwriting.

3. Math and Morning Room Time

   As explained in the Morning Room Time chapter.

4. PE

   Examples might be time at the neighborhood pool during warm months. Outdoor time, walking the trail, riding bikes and/or running and kicking the ball in the backyard.

5. Finish up the 3 Rs

6. Lunch

7. One More Thing After Lunch (or How We Fit in All the Extras)

8. Afternoon Quiet Time for Multiple Ages

   This is often when older children enjoy reading for pleasure or some history reading. Younger ones can also read or play quietly. See the Afternoon Quiet Time chapter.

9. Jurisdictions and Service Opportunities

   Because I can't possibly follow behind five children and keep the house picked up.

10. Technology for All Ages – The privilege of computer time

    Sometimes the children are rewarded with some screen time immediately following their Before 8:45 time in the morning. (If those things are done well.) And, of course, we use the computer for learning as needed throughout the school day for research and math time.

Hodgepodge Hint: Build your schedule in a way that is best for your family. Group extracurricular activities on one or two days so that you have plenty of time to *home*school.

Unit Studies with Multiple Ages

Unit studies are great for an age range because everyone is immersed in the same subject. Unit studies are often how we fit it all in! After the 3 Rs, we can mostly finish up the remainder of our subjects all together – all ages.

What is a unit study?

A unit study, in my words, is a thorough investigation of one topic – using living books, hands on projects, notebooking and more. For us, it is a lasagna approach – layering the learning. A unit study often is a suggestion or jumping off place for more research. You can just do a search at your library on one subject you want to study and you will find books for every age. Readers and story books for young ones, chapter books for older ones, living books for the whole family.

Here are a few more examples of unit study type approaches you can use with all of your ages:

Nature Study

Nature study is for all ages. No requirements. No prerequisites. Really, all we have to do is step outside. We don't have to stop and analyze what is best for each age.

The Gentle Ways of Reading

Older ones helping younger ones learn to read – I often ask the older children to read to the younger ones. Six-year-old loves to read to four-year-old. Mother Goose is not only good for the littlest ones, the rhyming is perfect reading practice. Plus just fun.

Read Alouds – of course this almost goes without mentioning but the benefits of reading aloud to the whole family are far-reaching. Even Mama learns something. Memories are made.

Games and online apps can often be great phonics and language practice.

Writing for an Age Range

- Making homemade books – this is a creative project for older children or for the one learning to read.
- Thank you notes – oh what a good practice this is – not only in letter writing but in gratitude. At Christmas we write a family thank you note – multiple ages – each one writing a line or two of thanks in one note to the recipient. This is a simple idea for gratitude, handwriting and art – for even the most reluctant writer.
- Handwriting and penmanship around the table – youngest ones can sketch, older ones write – each according to their skill level.
- Play-writing – sometimes for our history assignment, the children write a play set in the time period we are studying. Some play a role, some perform the videography duties.

Math for Multiple Ages

Marvelous math lessons can be accomplished on many levels with multiple ages – in several ways. Simple ideas like estimating popcorn, playing card games and counting everything you see!

So, while each child needs daily practice in the three Rs, you can enjoy these basics – all ages together.

Hodgepodge Hint: By using unit studies, the children can all learn together. The prep work is done for me. All I need to do is add the books and supplies called for. The end result is we add in so much more learning!

The Imperfect Homeschool: Drama and Trauma All the Time

"Your homeschool looks so peaceful."

"Wow, I wish I was as organized as you."

"Well, you have experience with teaching an age-range of children, I could never accomplish as much as you do."

Every now and then when I speak at conference or share online, I will get a comment like those above. I always think to myself… if only they *knew* the **drama** and **trauma** that goes on here daily. Also, remember that with social media posts that inundate our lives, you only witness the "perfect." You never get all the sensory overload that is happening at the time. The noise!

Drama and Trauma All The Time

Friends, homeschooling is refinement by fire. Daily, sometimes hourly, we have character issues we have to address. And with five children, there is just always something going on. An adjustment to make. And when that challenge is tackled, then there's something new to concentrate our prayers on.

Drama – we have three girls. Need I say more? Trauma – someone needing a band-aid, help finding a pair of socks – or my favorite homeschool daily – finding a pencil with an eraser. Drama and trauma all the time with five children.

Why So Positive Most of the Time?

- A few points. I do not write about my children's failings or speak poorly about them. Not because that doesn't ever happen but because I fail and make poor choices as well. We are human. A family all piled up together most of the time is bound to lose patience and struggle in one area or another.

- I also consider that, one day, when they are each much older, what might they find if they were to Google search their own name? Would words I write now somehow wound them in the future? That would never be my intention. I aim to show my love for them through my posts and to encourage other families.

- I count gifts. The Lord blesses us every day if only we will stop and take notice. So, yes, I do tend to share the highlights, the good, the accomplishments. But I do hope that you will see that we are an imperfect homeschool, a "we're working on it" sort of family. We struggle. And thank God He's not finished with us yet.

Most importantly, I can only do this through Him. Without Him I would be nothing. Without Him I'd surely fail…

Hodgepodge Hint: This bright, new day, complete with twenty-four hours of opportunities, choices, and attitudes comes with a perfectly matched set of 1,440 minutes. This unique gift, this one day, cannot be exchanged, replaced, or refunded. Handle with care. Make the most of it. There is only one to a customer! ~ Ellie Claire

Homeschooling High School Habits

The high school years are among the best of all of our homeschooling years. Because there are experts to help you in this area, I am sharing some simple encouragement and the habits that bless us the most. I know I was nervous and excited about the homeschooling high school adventure. I hung tightly to this encouraging quote as we started the first freshman year. Now we have two high school graduates and I have seen the results.

> **Hodgepodge Hint:** *God does not ask your ability or your inability. He asks only your availability. ~ Mary Kay Ash*

Widening of Course Load and Transcript Keeping. Honestly, I did not notice a huge difference from the homeschooling aspect except maybe in work load. My student's workload and mine. There is a widening of course work, experiments, writing assignments and *a whole lot of books*. There is more planning required for the homeschool parent. There is transcript keeping and credits to consider. There are also many ways to homeschool high school! How wonderful that you can homeschool traditionally, you can add in online courses and even take classes outside classes at umbrella and public high schools.

Offer Quiet Working Spaces. Give your high schoolers the gift of learning space in the midst of a busy household. Maybe set up a desk tucked into the corner of a bedroom or another quiet area of your home. Much of high school is independent work. You are overseeing the course work, having discussions and keeping track of courses and credits. Your student may need to curl up with a textbook or current assignment and read.

In summary

We follow a college preparatory course of study in our homeschool. We do this not because we are certain that each of our children is headed to college. We follow this course because we know that a rigorous four year plan will not only challenge our students but prepare them in case the Lord does have a college path in His plans. Ultimately, *I have no greater joy than to hear that my children are walking in the truth.* 3 John 1:4

Homeschooling High School Credits

My friend Sherri explained high school credits this way. When your student complete 75% of a textbook, that is a credit. A standard school year on one course equals a credit. A half of a year would be a half credit. Most public schools require four English credits, four Math credits, four Science credits, three Social Studies credits, two Foreign Language credits, one Physical Education, and one Health. The balance of the credits required for graduation is for Electives of your child's choice. I encourage you to explore your state requirements for high school graduation. You should also explore the homeschooling high school section of the Home School Legal Defense Association (HSLDA).

Put together a high school transcript. My daughter's first choice in a college had a homeschool transcript template we downloaded and filled out. So, check with the colleges your student is interested in. Click on that 'homeschool' tab!

Start writing course descriptions. They may not be necessary. But in all my research and in taking the advice of seasoned homeschoolers, I believe this is the way to go. Even if a college does not request course descriptions. (See resource section)

Spend time in the sophomore and junior years on SAT/ACT test prep. Schedule taking the SAT and/or ACT late junior and senior years.

Homeschooling High School Shifting of Roles

One of the grand balancing acts is that of being both a parent *and* a homeschool teacher. Add in the need for being the high school guidance counselor and a homeschool parent can be stressed. I find myself sometimes wishing that I could simply fall into one of those roles. And it is at those times that I pull myself aside for a homeschool parent teacher conference. Yes, just a little talk with myself. A rest. A breather. But mostly a focus on the Lord – *asking for His wisdom and provision.*

Talk to a fellow homeschool mother you know. We are not meant to go on this homeschool journey alone but to encourage each other. Send an email, set a coffee date or make a phone call.

> **Hodgepodge Hint:** Have fun. I see and hear so many 'you need tos' and pieces of advice out there. But I am here to say it just does not need to be hard work all the time. Be sure to add in some fun. Plan for fun if you need to!

The Imperfect Homeschooler's Guide to the College Search

Deep breath. You've reached it – the college search. As a homeschool parent, the college search may have seemed so far off. It certainly did for me. However, it is fantastic journey to be on with your high schooler. My high schoolers and I have learned a few things. We are still learning. Still stepping out into unknown territory. But it is exciting! And the Lord has every step in His most capable hands.

Tips for the Homeschooler's College Search

The Lord has plans for each of our children. Yes, we have made sure that our homeschool high school is a college preparatory one. Because we wanted to be sure that was definitely an option. Is college always the best route for a homeschool graduate? Not always. Our second high school graduate is doing studies online and taking an entrepreneurial approach.

Don't be so serious! (Speaking to myself here). It is so very easy to get caught up in all the 'need to' and compare ourselves to other families on the college search. To remedy this, we decided that on every college trip we would make sure we also simply had FUN. A quick side trip to a local spot, a hike and maybe a stop for apples.

Don't fret. The majority of colleges are homeschool friendly. Both of the student guides we have toured around with were either homeschooled or had homeschool connections. The colleges we have been in contact with are very homeschool friendly.

Visit! Go to those colleges. Ask questions. Have fun. Our experience has been fantastic. These colleges have admissions students who are trained and so very helpful. These students will call, text and they will meet you at admissions when you arrive. They love what they do.

If you can, we definitely suggest you sit in on a college class. We did and it were able to speak with the college professor and ask questions afterwards. We also ate lunch in the cafeteria. Take advantage of any or all of these as you visit college campuses.

Set attainable goals. When I was writing course descriptions, I decided I would work 15 minutes a day for a week. Your high schooler could have a our simple goal to do "one adult thing each week." That might be applying for a scholarship or making a phone call to a college to ask a question. So much can be accomplished with just a little bit of daily investment.

Cherish this time! It goes so fast, friends.

> **Hodgepodge Hint:** Lean on other homeschool parents that have gone before you. Those that 'know'. Surround yourself with others who are several steps ahead of you and/or on the same journey.

Thank you

Thank you to my fun, Hodgepodge family for being a picture of enduring love, making me laugh often and making this life so rich. You have stepped in and stepped up and served in countless ways.

To my mama, Nana, thank you for always reminding me that I AM an artist.

Many thanks to my long-time friends and homeschool mentors. I so appreciate the time you invested in my life to encourage me and build my confidence to homeschool. Thank you for keeping me from not pulling my hair out early on, for modeling wonderful Christian homes and for helping us grow the Godly Habits outlined in the pages of this book.

I'm so grateful for the encouragement and support of my blogging friends. Thank you for helping me break through my introverted ways.

A heap of gratitude goes to my excellent friends and editors, for their gentle urging, expertise and skill.

To my husband, Steve, thank you for your Godly leadership, all of our daily adventures, your listening ear and for date nights.

About Our Hodgepodge

We've been homeschooling for almost 20 years now. Homeschooling all these years has definitely been a healthy dose of both fun and chaos. My husband and I have five children. In our homeschool, we have an age range of children from elementary up to high school. We have had 17 years of preschoolers! So far we have celebrated two homeschool graduates – one is a college student and one is taking online studies with an entrepreneurial track. It is always a hodgepodge.

About Tricia

Tricia is the founder of Hodgepodge where she shares helpful habits, art lessons plus allergy-friendly recipes and simple strategies for the day to day. With their You ARE an Artist curriculum at ChalkPastel.com, she, her mother "Nana", and her family are passionate about helping others growing a love of art. It's a multi-generational, around-the-table, all-together style of art. Tricia also writes reviews of her family's favorite homeschool curriculum at The Curriculum Choice. She helps others build healthy habits with her Families of Wellness community. Find it all at hodgepodgemom.com.

Tricia and the Hodgepodge live in Georgia where they love to explore local hiking trails, the Georgia coast and the rich southern history.

Favorite Resources

Find clickable links to all of these resources at

www.hodgepodge.me/book-extras

365 Days of Celebration and Praise, Julie Lavender

A Plan in Place homeschool planners

A Reason for Handwriting

Advent storybook series by Arnold Ytreeide

Alphaphonics curriculum

Apologia curriculum

Audubon First Field Guides

Answers in Genesis

Before Five in a Row

Compass Classroom curriculum

Comprehensive Record Solution

Creative Family Times

Do Hard Things, Alex and Brett Harris

Doorposts' A Checklist for Parents

Duggar family

Educating the Whole-Hearted Child

Everyday Homemaking, Vicki Bentley

Explode the Code curriculum

Five in Row curriculum

Flylady household habits

Handbook of Nature Study curriculum

Harmony Fine Arts curriculum

Homeschool Mommy Marks and Universities, Annie Kate

Homeschooling for College By Design, Heather Woodie

Homeschooling Gifted and Advanced Learners, Cindy West

Homeschooling High School By Design, Heather Woodie

Homeschooling High School with College in Mind, Betsy Sproger

Homeschooling Methods and Philosophies, at The Curriculum Choice

Homeschooling Today Magazine

Home School Legal Defense Association (HSLDA)

HSLDA Homeschooling the Early Years, Vicki Bentley

I Saw the Angel in the Marble, Chris and Ellyn Davis

IKEA furniture

Leading Little Ones to God, Marian M. Schoolland

Loving Living Math, Our Journey Westward

Manners Made Easy, June Hines Moore

NaturExplorers curriculum, Our Journey Westward

Parenting the Early Years, Drs. Les and Leslie Parrott

Power of Praying for Your Adult Children, Stormie Omartian

Outdoor Hour Challenges, Barb McCoy

Outgrowing the Greenhouse, Gregg Harris Rod and Staff Books

Slow and Steady Get Me Ready curriculum

Sonlight curriculum

Spelling Workout curriculum

SQUILT Music curriculum

Tapestry of Grace curriculum

Teaching Textbooks curriculum

The Way They Learn, Cynthia Tobias

Unit Studies by Amanda Bennett curriculum

Well Trained Mind, The, Susan Wise Bauer

You Are Special Today plate

Your Morning Basket, Pam Barnhill

Made in the USA
Coppell, TX
19 November 2022